MW01241354

The Promise

The Promise

Renae Johnson

ISBN: 978-0-692-80538-1

Renae The Waitress, LLC
PO Box 210796
Nashville, TN 37221

1-800-820-5405
www.RenaetheWaitress.com

Special Thanks to Steve at Red Inc. for his faithful support and talent in creating such great books. Plus.....I really like you !!

And last but not least *Thank You* artists and cast of Larry's Country Diner for being apart of a show that brings honor to the LORD.

Other books by Renae Johnson
Diary of a TV Waitress
Precious Memories Memorial
Precious Memories Legacy

Introduction

Don't Forget the PROMISE

How many times have you heard that said on our TV show *Larry's Country Diner?* It is one of the important pieces of this crazy Diner show that seems to have no structure. Much like our daily lives reading the Promise becomes the one moment in time we take a breath and listen to what God is saying to us.

Promises at the Diner have come in a box, a desk holder, and a ceramic loaf of bread and even color-coded. I thought the color coded Promises would keep Larry from reading the same promise the next time. But if you watch our show, it didn't help a bit.

Our musical guests on the Diner seem to really enjoy that segment…a novelty from the other shows they perform on. And the patrons in the Diner itself feel it's a blanket blessing for their food. I am not sure that is actually biblical…?

But the Promise is God's living word and can be applied to wherever and whatever we are doing in our lives. Promises fill us with hope when we feel hopeless and bring joy when there seems to be nothing to smile about and peace in the middle of turmoil. Which seems to be the Diner a lot of times.

The PROMISES in this book were read on one of *Larry's Country Diner* TV shows over the past 7 years. It includes a photo of the artist and the airdate of the show.

I hope you are blessed with **THE PROMISE** and the different translations.

Renae the Waitress
www.renaethewaitress.com

Contents

Rhonda Vincent

Ed Bruce

Gary Morris

His name

ing

Psalm 149:3

Justin Trevino

Mo Pitney

Sylvia

Doyle Dykes

Psalm 43:3

Send out thy light and thy truth,

let ME lead them.

Dan Miller | aired 4/11/14

Isaiah 62:4

The Lord delighteth in thee.

The Roy's | aired 5/12/11

Psalms 23:3

He restoreth my soul.

He leadeth me in the paths of

righteousness for His namesake.

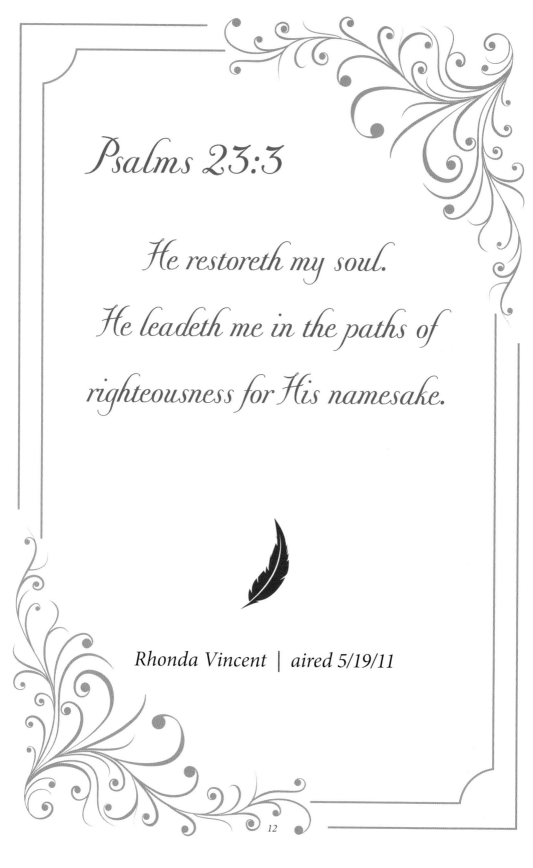

Rhonda Vincent | aired 5/19/11

Numbers 6:25

My face will shine upon you

all the days of your life.

Proverbs 17:22

A Merry Heart doeth good like a medicine.

Jean Shepard | aired 6/2/11

Psalms 103:2

Bless the Lord all

my soul and forget

not all of his benefits.

The Cleverlys' | *aired 5/26/11*

2 Corinthians 9:8

God is able to make all grace

abound toward you.

Buck Trent | aired 9/15/11

2 John 1:3

Grace be with you,
mercy and peace from God.

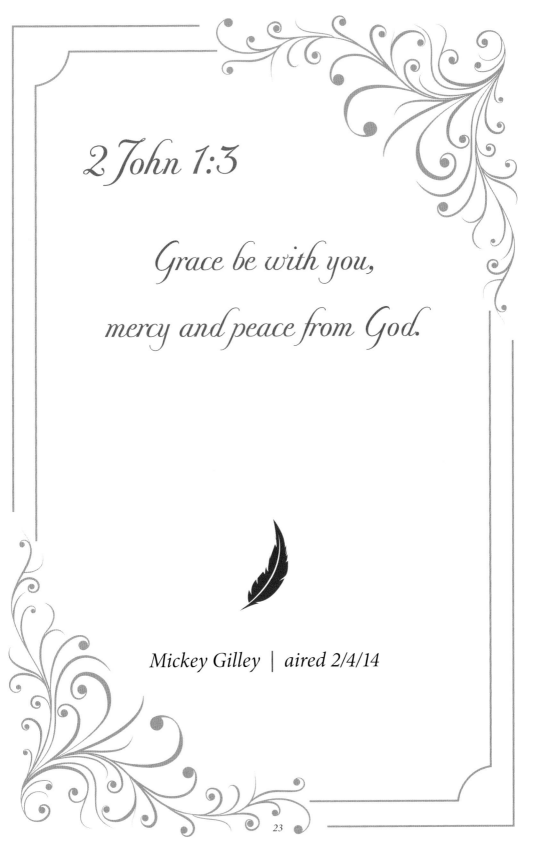

Mickey Gilley | aired 2/4/14

Psalm 37:18

All your days are known to

Me and your inheritance

is secure forever.

Psalm 118:24

This is the day,
which the Lord has made.
We will rejoice and be glad in it.

Exile | aired 10/6/11

Psalm 146:2

While I live,
will I praise the Lord.

Jimmy C Newman | aired 10/13/11

Psalm 16:11

In thy presence is fullness of joy.
At thou right hand there are
pleasures forever more.

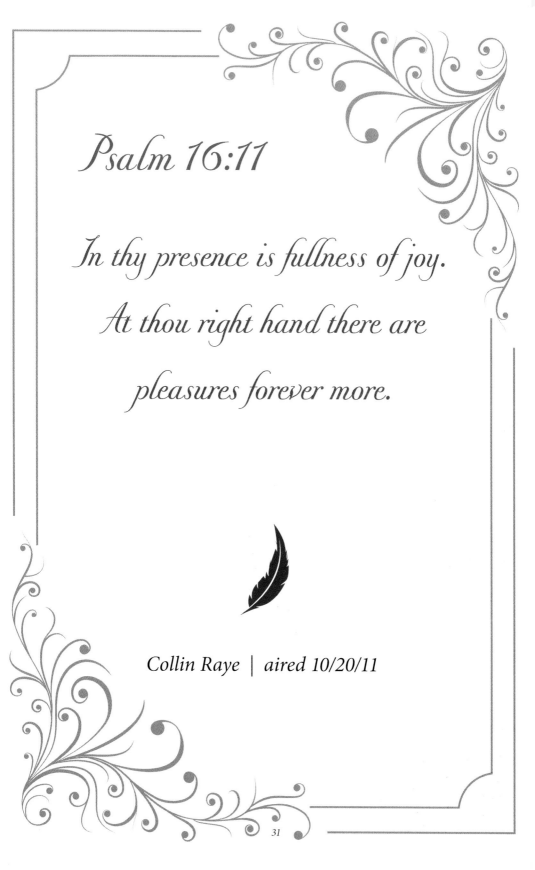

Collin Raye | aired 10/20/11

2 Corinthians 13:11

The God of love and peace

shall be with you.

Leona Williams | aired 10/17/11

Titus 1:2

You can rest in MY promise
of eternal life, for I cannot lie.

Psalm 7:17

I will give thanks to the Lord because of his righteousness and will sing praise to the name of the Lord most high.

Ed Bruce | aired 11/19/09

Psalms 37:4

Delight thyself also in the Lord
and he will give thee the
desires of your heart.

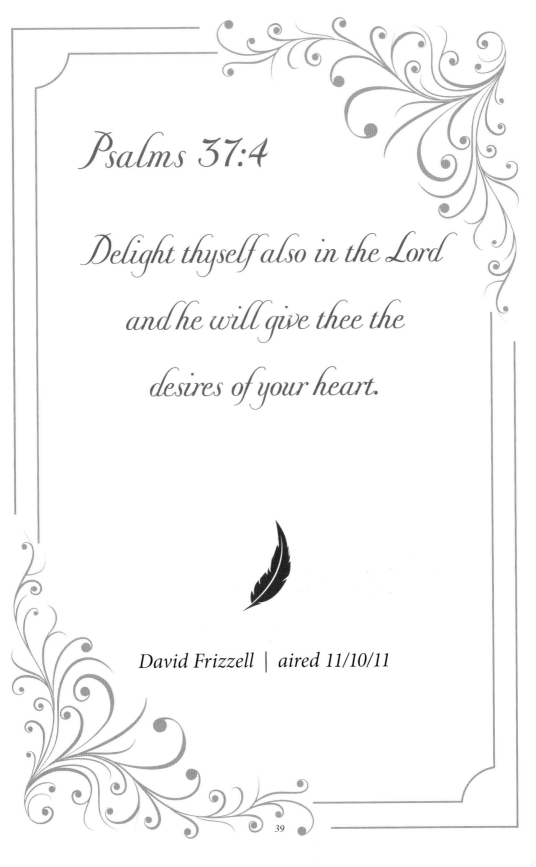

David Frizzell | aired 11/10/11

Psalms 98:4

Make a joyful noise

unto the Lord.

Make a loud noise and rejoice.

Janie Fricke | aired 12/29/11

Psalm 113:3

From the rising of the sun unto

the going down of the same,

the Lord's name is to

be praised.

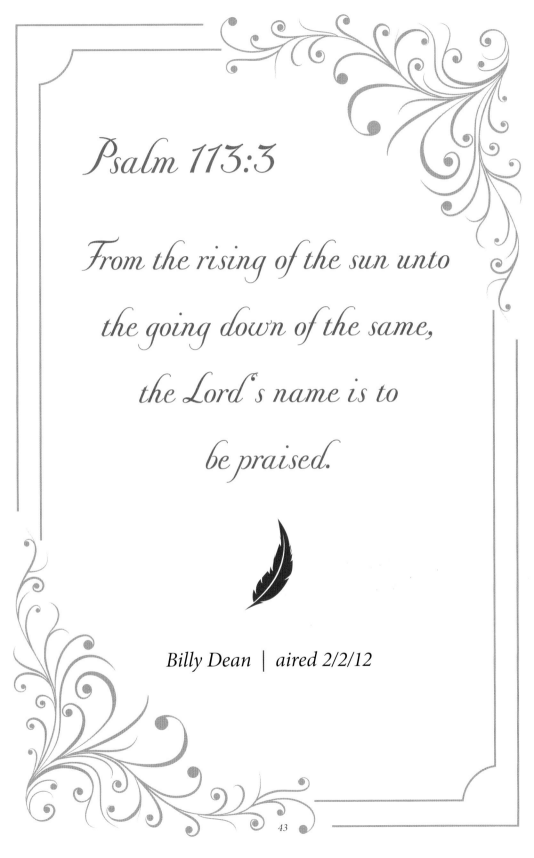

Billy Dean | aired 2/2/12

Job 33:4

My Spriit made you and
My breath gives you life.

Isaiah 61:10

I will greatly rejoice in the Lord.

My soul shall be joyful in my God.

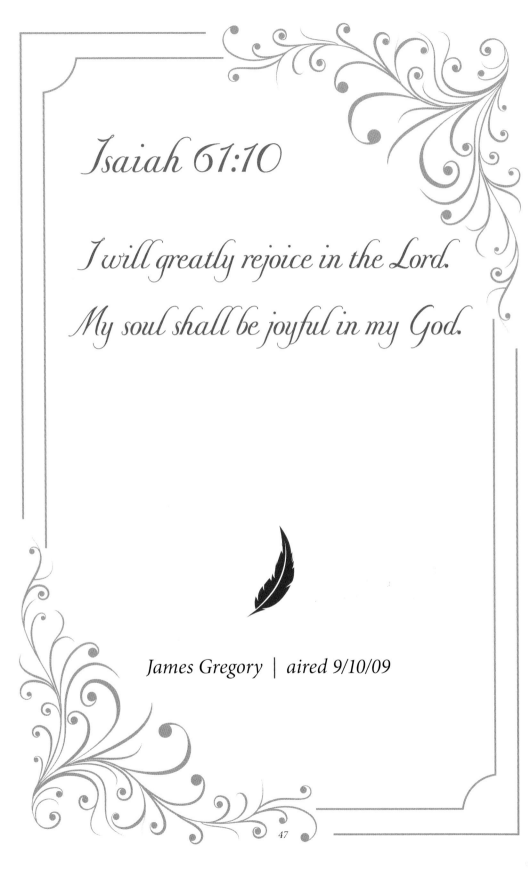

James Gregory | aired 9/10/09

Psalm 150:6

Let everything that has

breath praise the Lord.

Bill Anderson | aired 9/5/09

Deuteronomy 26:11

Thou shall rejoice in every good thing which the Lord they God has given unto thee.

Gene Watson | aired 10/15/09

2 Peter 3:18

Grow in grace and in the knowledge of our Lord and savior Jesus Christ.

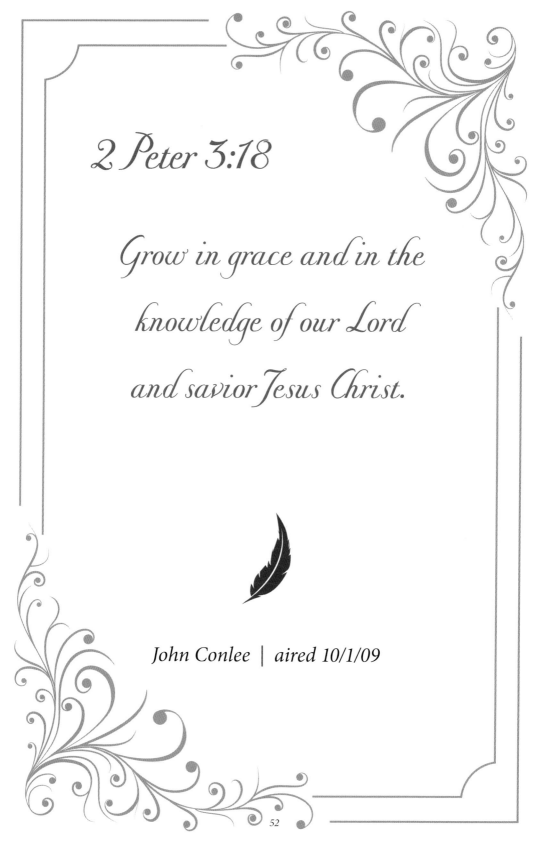

John Conlee | aired 10/1/09

Galatians 5:22

The Fruit of the Spirit is love, joy and peace.

Jeannie Seely | aired 10/22/09

Malachi 3:6

I am the Lord your God

and I never change.

Luke 1:37

With God

nothing shall be impossible.

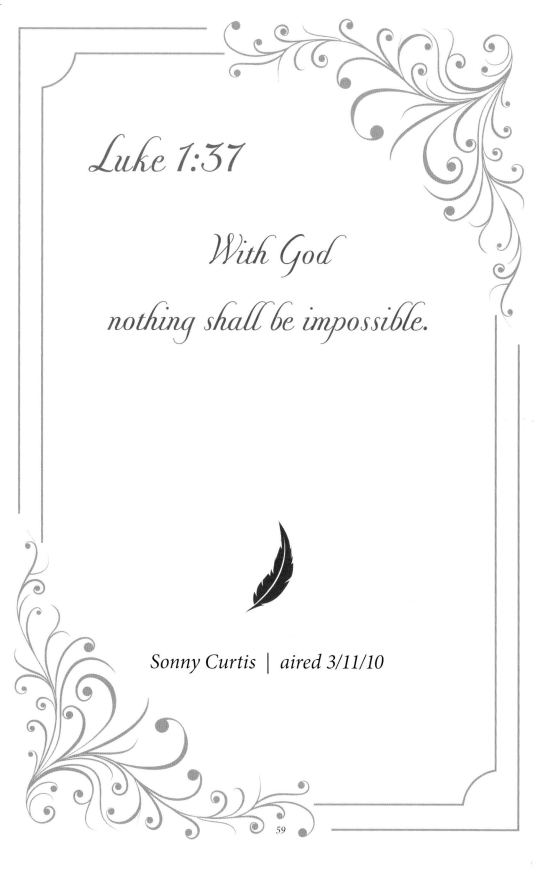

Sonny Curtis | aired 3/11/10

Psalm 107:9

He satisfies the longing

soul and filleth the

hungry soul with goodness.

Jim Ed Brown | aired 10/29/09

Psalm 33:21

Thou art my hope oh God.

Thou are my trust

from my youth.

Riders In The Sky | *aired 3/18/10*

Mathew 28:20

I am with you always.

Gary Morris | aired 4/1/10

Psalm 96:1

Give unto the Lord Glory

and Strength.

Give unto the Lord the glory

due unto his name.

Mandy Barnett | aired 4/15/10

Joshua 23:14

Not one of My promises
will ever fail you.

1 Chronicles 16:37

Glory and Honor

are in his presence.

Strength and gladness

are in his place.

Time Jumpers | aired 5/13/10

Psalm 3:3

Thou Oh Lord are

the shield for me.

The glory and

the lifter of mine head.

Moe Bandy | aired 11/28/10

Romans 8:37

We are more than conquerors

through him that loved us.

Billy Grammer | aired 12/10/10

Psalm 51:10

Create in me a clean heart

oh God and renew a right spirit

within me.

Dallas Fraiser | aired 12/24/10

Psalm 62:7

In God is my salvation,

and my glory, the rock of my

strength and my refuge is in God.

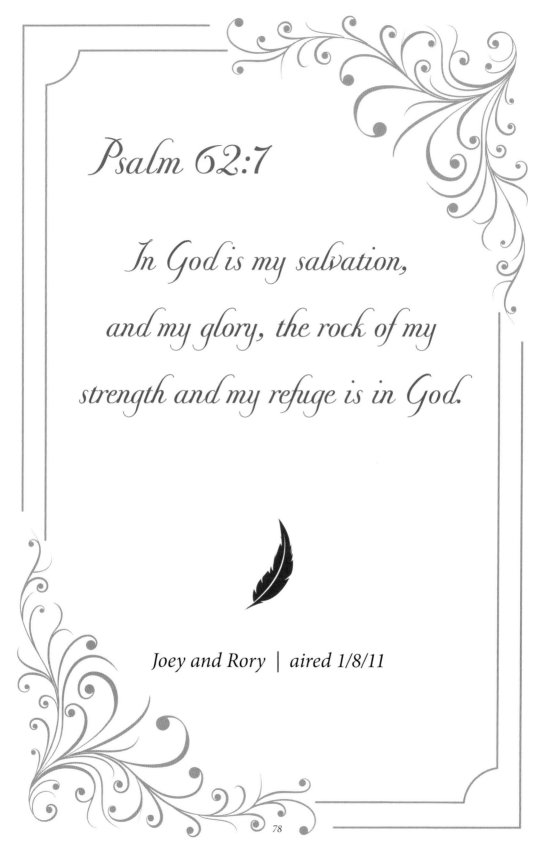

Joey and Rory | aired 1/8/11

Timothy 6:17

The living God gives us richly

all things to enjoy.

Justin Trevino | aired 1/29/11

Matthew 7:7

Ask and it shall be given you. Seek and ye shall find, knock and it shall be opened to you.

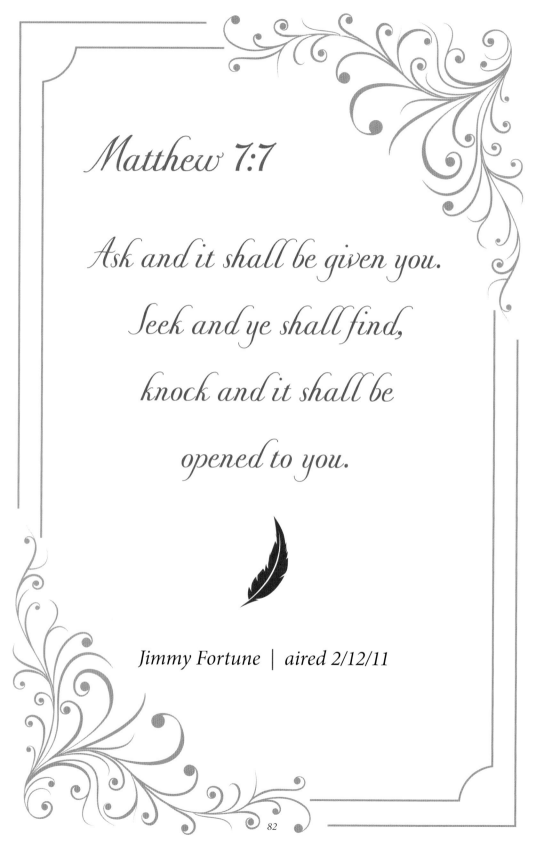

Jimmy Fortune | aired 2/12/11

Psalm 28:7

The Lord is my strength
and my shield.
My heart trusted in him
and I am helped.

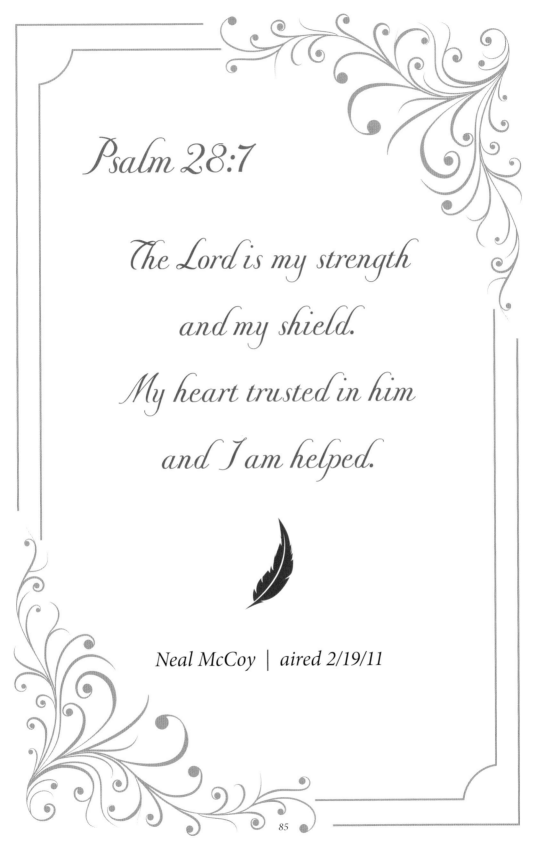

Neal McCoy | aired 2/19/11

Proverbs 25:11

A word fitly spoken

is like apples of gold

in pictures of sliver.

Con Hunley | aired 3/5/11

John 10:10

I am come, that they might have life and that they might have it more abundantly.

Suzy Bogguss | aired 3/26/11

Psalm 57:1

My soul trusteth in thee,

in the shadow of thy wings

will I make my refuge.

Dailey and Vincent | aired 4/11/13

Psalm 36:15

Thy mercy Oh Lord is in the

heavens and they faithfulness

reacheth unto the clouds.

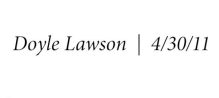

Doyle Lawson | 4/30/11

Acts 17:27

Reach out and you

will touch Me,

for I am not far from you.

Psalm 27:5

He will hide me in the
shelter of his tabernacle and
set me upon a high rock.

The Oak Ridge Boys | 6/28/12

Isaiah 26:3

Thou will keep

in perfect peace whose mind

is stayed on thee.

The Whites | *aired 7/19/12*

Deuteronomy 33:12

The beloved of the Lord

shall dwell in the safety by him

and the Lord shall cover him

all the day long.

LaDonna Gatlin | aired 9/27/12

Ephesians 4:2

Be completely humble and gentle. Be patient, bearing with one another in love.

Mo Pitney | aired 1/24/13

Joel 2:21

Be glad and rejoice,

for the Lord will do

great things.

1 Peter 1:15, 16

Just as he who called you is holy, so be holy in all you do. For it is written be holy, because I am holy.

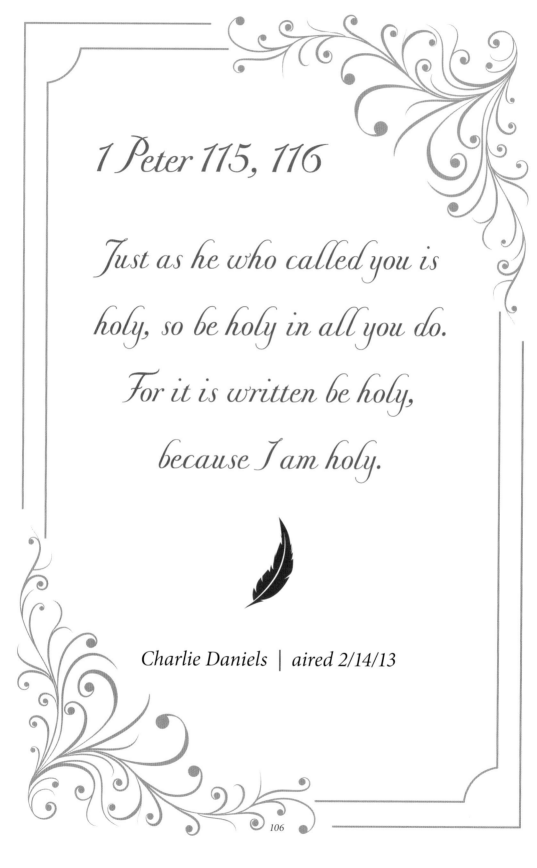

Charlie Daniels | aired 2/14/13

Philippians 4:8

Whatever is true, whatever is noble, whatever is right, whatever is pure, whatever is lovely, whatever is admirable, think about such things.

The Church Sisters | 2/21/13

Psalm 29:11

The Lord will give

strength unto his people.

The Lord will bless his people

with peace.

Roy Clark | aired 3/26/13

Romans 15:13

Now the God of hope

will you all with

joy and peace believing.

Billy Yates | aired 6/3/13

2 John 1:3

Grace be with you, mercy, and peace, from God.

Ecclesiastes 3:11

He hath made everything

beautiful in his time.

Jim Glaser | 8/17/13

Psalm 71:5

You have been my hope,

oh Lord, my confidence

since my youth.

Tracy Lawrence | aired 8/24/13

Psalm 119:14

Thou art my hiding place.

Thou shall preserve me

from trouble.

Vince Gill | aired 5/2/15

Matthew 5:6

Blessed are those who hunger and thirst for righteousness, for they will be filled.

Crystal Gayle | aired 3/28/15

1 Samuel 12:22

I will not abandon you,

for I am glad to make you

My very own.

Lamentations 3:22

For his compassions never fail,

they are new every morning.

Jason Crabb | aired 5/2/15

Psalm 77:2

In the day of my trouble

I will call on thee,

for thou wilt answer me.

Sylvia | 8/15/15

Psalm 68:19

Blessed be the Lord who daily

loadeth us with benefits,

even the God of our salvation.

Teea Goans | *aired 4/18/15*

Galatians 3:29

If you belong to Christ,

then you are Abraham's seed,

and heirs according to

the promise.

Ronnie McDowell | *aired 2/21/15*

John 15:9

As the Father hath love me,

so have I loved you:

continue ye in my love.

John Anderson | aired 3/3/16

Proverbs 18:10

My name is a strong

tower that you can run to

and find safety.

John 12:16

If any man serve me,

him will my Father honor.

Darrell McCall | 4/28/16

Matthew 5:8

Blessed are the pure of
heart for they shall see God.

The Malpass Brothers | aired 7/14/16

John 6:37

All that the Father gives me will come to me, and whoever comes to me I will never cast out.

The Texas Tenors | 3/24/16

Proverbs 2:6

For the Lord gives wisdom;

from his mouth come knowledge

and understanding.

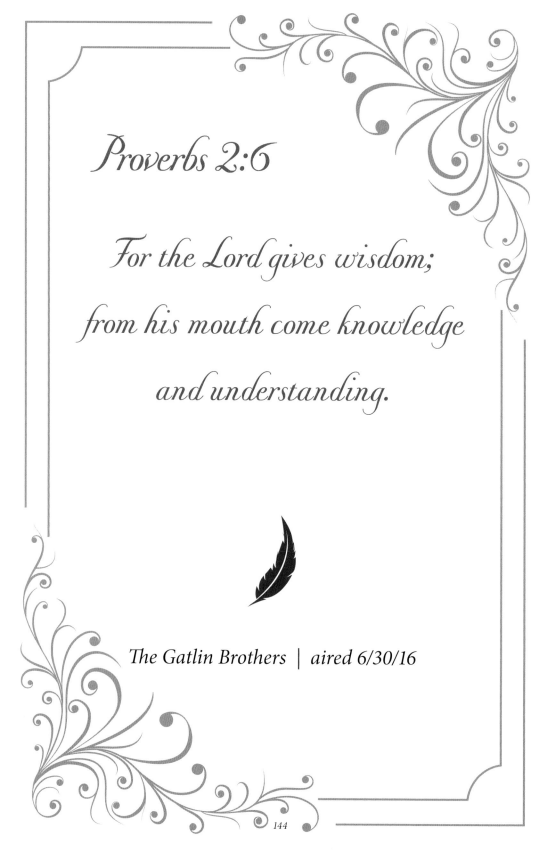

The Gatlin Brothers | aired 6/30/16

Hebrew 4:16

Let us therefore come boldly

into the throne of Grace that we

may obtain mercy and find grace

to help in time of need.

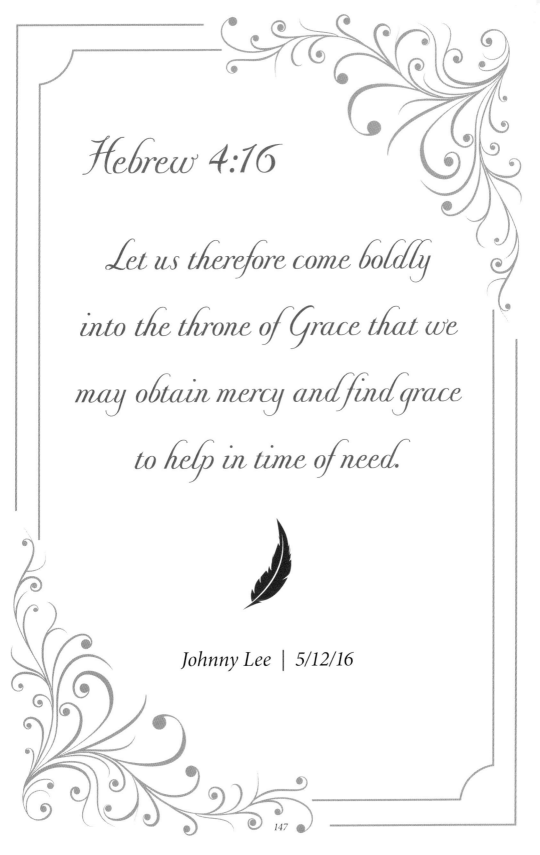

Johnny Lee | 5/12/16

Hebrews 13:5

Never will I leave you;

Never will I forsake you.

Ricky Skaggs and
Sharon White | aired 12/1/14

Revelation 3:20

I stand at the door, and knock:
if any man hear my voice, and open
the door, I will come in to him, and
will sup with him, and he with me.

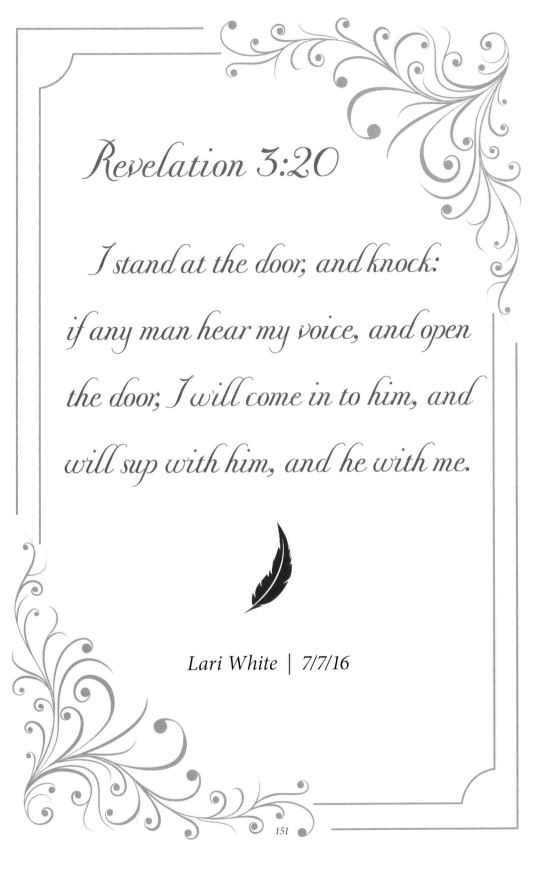

Lari White | 7/7/16

James 4:8

Draw near to God,

and He will draw near to you.

Psalm 34:7

The angel of the LORD encamps

around those who fear him,

and he delivers them.

Gordon Mote | 2/14/16

Matthew 5:7

Blessed are the merciful,

for they will shown mercy.

John Berry | aired 9/8/16

Deuteronomy 33:27

The eternal God is your refuge,

and underneath are the

ever lasting arms.

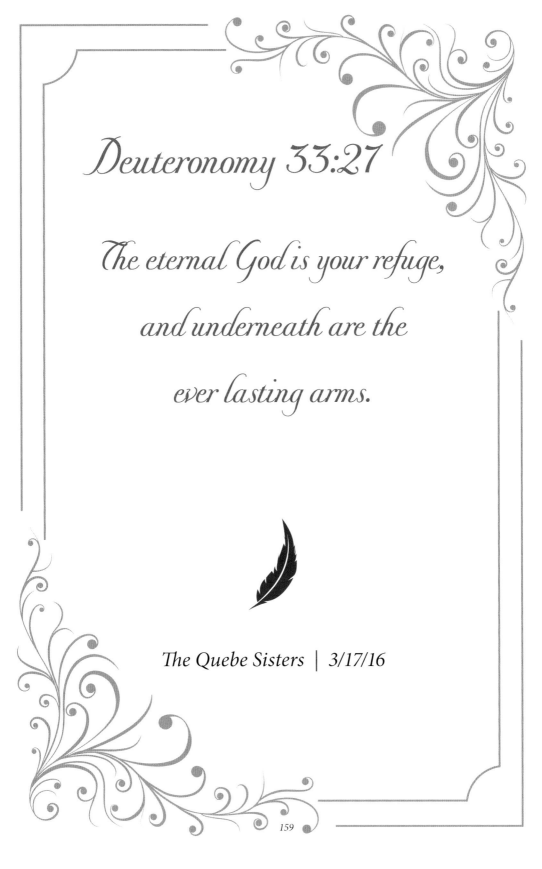

The Quebe Sisters | 3/17/16

Matthew 6:4

So that your giving may be in secret, then shall your Father, who sees what is done in secret, will reward you.

George Hamilton IV | aired 8/30/14

Isaiah 58:10

If you pour yourself out for the hungry and satisfy the needs of the afflicted, then shall your light rise in the darkness.

Doyle Dykes | 5/5/16

Philippians 4:4

Rejoice in the Lord always.

Johnny Rodriguez | aired 8/3/14

Psalm 36:5

Your love, Lord, reaches

to the heavens, your faithfulness

to the skies.

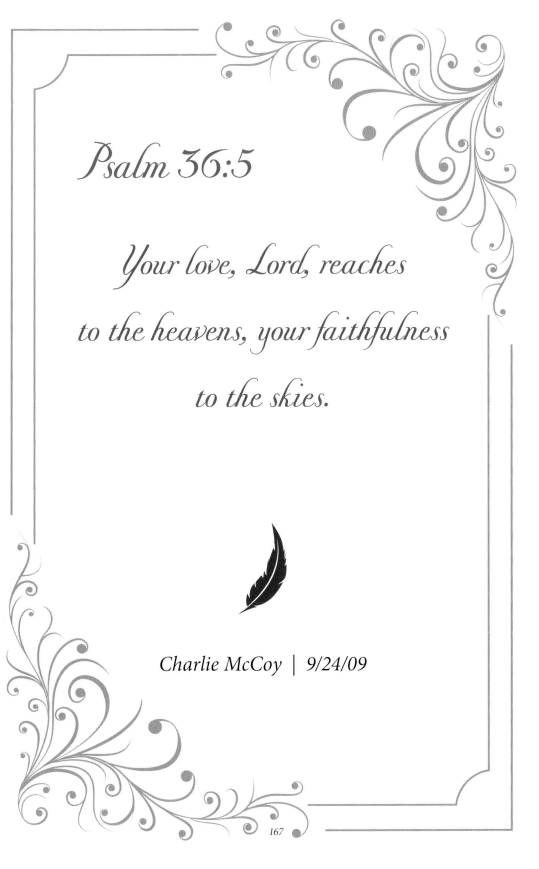

Charlie McCoy | 9/24/09

More Books by Renae Johnson

Diary of a TV Waitress

Sharing the fun of being a TV waitress on a top rated television show is why I wrote this book. I have answered a zillion questions over the years from "Is that your real hair color?" to "Is Nadine a man?" Not only do I answer all of these questions but also I share the on-the-show experiences and behind-the-counter antics. If you are real Larry's Country Diner fan you will enjoy this book. *$24.95*

Precious Memories Memorial

A long awaited book by so many country music fans. It covers over 80 country music legends lives, deaths, and final resting places. When they died? How they died? And who attended their funerals? And photos and maps of their final resting places. You will learn about Jimmy Dean being placed in a 9-½ foot long, granite piano-shape mausoleum over looking the James River. And Faron Young's ashes being spread behind Johnny Cash's home. This 248 page hard cover book has become a best seller with country music fans. *$24.95*

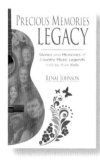

Precious Memories LEGACY

I refer to this book as the companion book to *Precious Memories Memorial*. It contains stories and memories from the *Kids* of some of these Country Music Legends. I interviewed 19 of the kids and asked them all the same questions, but the answers were all different. I wanted to know if they resented the fans for the time lost with their parents? What kind of friends did they have? What "stars" hung around at their house? What do you miss most about their parent? This book will make you laugh and make you cry as you hear from the KIDS. *$16.95*

Visit my website @ **Renaethewaitress.com** or available on Amazon.